THIS BOOK BELONGS TO

PRESENTED BY

DATE

Who Is This
JESUS?

For Daxon

Library of Congress Cataloging-in-Publication Data
Creek, Lorie, author.
    Who is this Jesus? a hidden picture book / illustrations by Christopher Creek; text by Lorie Creek.
        pages cm
    Summary: A hidden picture book about Jesus Christ.
    ISBN 978–1–60908–909–2 (hardbound : alk. paper)
    1. Jesus Christ. 2. Picture books for children. 3. Picture puzzles.
    I. Creek, Christopher H., illustrator. II. Title.
    BT303.C84 2012
    232—dc23   2011043929

Printed in Mexico
R. R. Donnelley, Reynosa, Mexico

10   9   8   7   6   5   4   3   2   1

Who Is This
JESUS?

A HIDDEN PICTURE BOOK

Paintings by **Christopher Creek**

Written by **Lorie Creek**

ENSIGN
PEAK

He is the Good Shepherd protecting His lambs;

He tenderly calms with the touch of His hands.

Find the twelve hidden lambs.

He is the Prince and
His gospel is peace;

The lamb and the lion
both follow His lead.

Can you find the seven lambs and five lion cubs
walking along with the Savior?

He is the Savior
who rescues the one;

He will not rest 'til
His work is all done.

There are twenty-six hidden lambs to find and a heart shape,
signifying the love between the Savior and His lambs.

He is the Creator
of both great and small;

He tends as He reigns
and He watches them all.

Can you find eleven more of the Savior's creations?
There are two butterflies, a rabbit, a raccoon, an owl, a small bird,
a squirrel, an eagle, a cat, a deer, and a dog to find.

He is the Master
on whom we rely;

He always and faithfully
stays by our side.

Find a flock of at least twenty sheep,
a sleeping lost lamb, and a dog bone.

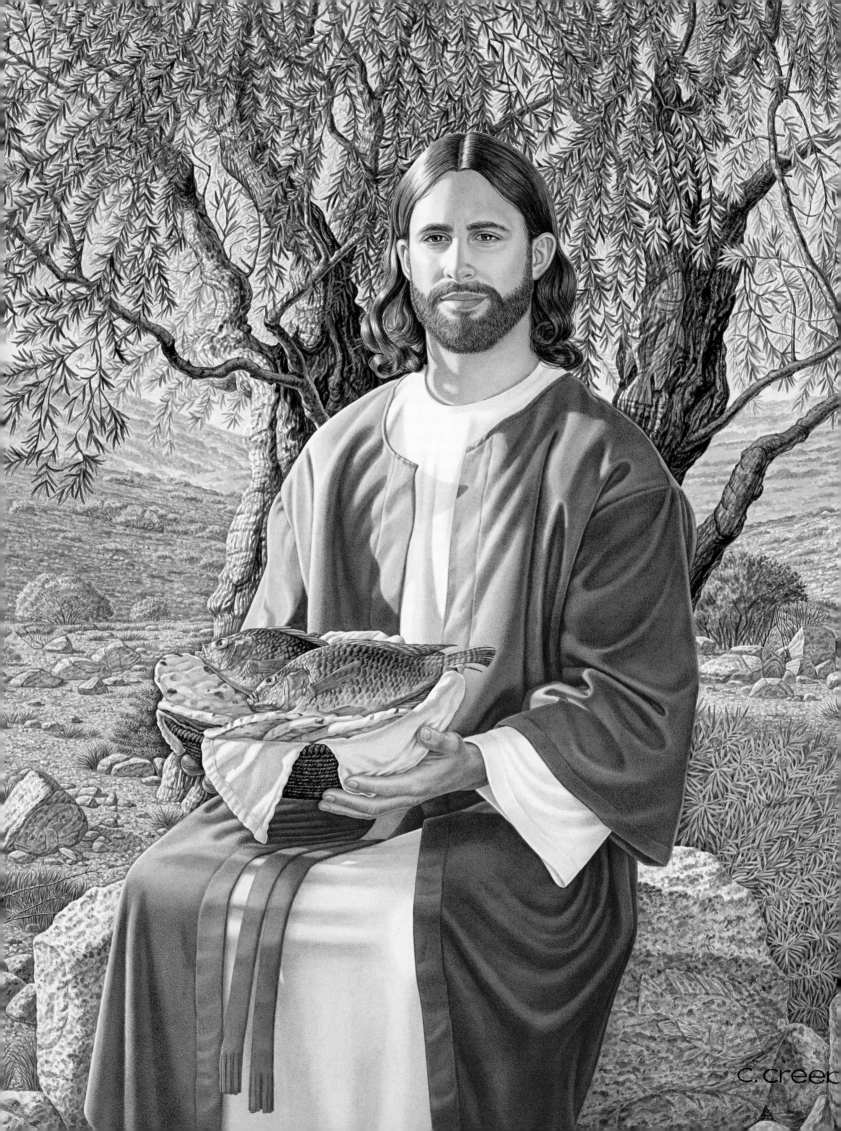

He is the Giver of all that is good;

He invites each to come feast on His word.

Find an additional ten loaves and ten fishes.

He is the Healer who cures us from ills;

He minds and He mends; He soothes and He stills.

Can you find the nine lepers who did not return to the Savior after being healed?

He is the Gatherer
of all that He made;

He calls to each gently
and knows them by name.

Find ten hidden chicks.

He is the Blessed Baby born so long ago;

He came from above to save us here below.

Hidden in the background is a trumpeting angel celebrating the birth of our Savior.

He is the Judge who
rules from on high;

He marked the path
and helps us choose right.

Find the four sheep on the Savior's right-hand side
and the four goats on His left.

He is the Friend
from beginning to end;

Everyone counts and
is priceless to Him.

There are ten hidden sparrows. Also look for a grasshopper,
a caterpillar, two ladybugs, a bird nest with three eggs,
a monarch butterfly, a damselfly, and a praying mantis.

His name is Jesus, the Lord God above;

He is our Everything! His name is Love.

Find nine additional doves ascending upward with the white dove.

About the Author and Illustrator

Chris and Lorie Creek have been married for twenty-eight years and are the parents of three sons. Chris received his bachelor's degree in fine art and illustration, and Lorie received her bachelor's degree in English and American literature. Chris has worked mainly as an artist and illustrator and recently retired from his computer-based art company to dedicate his full-time attention to painting. Lorie is a homemaker and also enjoys volunteer work. *Who Is This Jesus?* is their first book together. Chris's art is available at ChristopherCreekArt.com.